On Top of the World
Profiles in Courage
Women of the Nation of Islam

Dr. Toni. S. Muhammad

Foreword by
Nisa I. Muhammad

ISBN-13: 978-0985759254
ISBN-10: 0985759259

DEDICATION

For My Daughters, Tynetta & Ava, and all the girls reared in the teachings of the Most Honorable Elijah Muhammad as exemplified and taught by the Honorable Louis Farrakhan through the Muslim Girls Training & General Civilization Class. You stand on the shoulders of giants that you may see farther to go further. We Salute You!

Muhammad

CONTENTS

	Acknowledgments	1
	Foreword	3
1	In Health	7
2	In Education	33
3	In Arts & Culture	55
4	In Justice/Defense	79
5	In Agriculture/ Science	93
6	In Information	103
7	Spiritual Development	119
8	World Class Ambassadors & Leadership	135

"I can sit on top of the world and tell everyone that the most beautiful nation is in the wilderness of North America..."

Master Fard Muhammad

ACKNOWLEDGMENTS

"I wish you could see them," these words resonated with my soul when the Honorable Minister Louis Farrakhan spoke them in Washington, D.C., at the 20th anniversary of the Million Man March – 10-10-15! I thank Allah, for intervening in our affairs in the person of Master Fard Muhammad, and every day for raising the Most Honorable Elijah Muhammad, and for His Divine Reminder, the Honorable Minister Louis Farrakhan who continues to give so much divine inspiration to so many in this world. His work is profound and truly a guide on the straight path. During the historical program in front of the Capital, when the M.G.T. and G.C.C. (women in the Nation of Islam) took the stage, it was truly a glimpse of heaven on earth. On Top of the World is a small view into our lives.

I want to thank my husband for his tireless nudging, encouragement, and amazing conceptualization of this project. Our conversations opened doors in my mind that were closed. Thank you for being the F.O.I. (Fruit of Islam) that Allah has appointed to my life. I also want to express my most sincere gratitude to the most magnificent, truly courageous M.G.T. and G.C.C., those in this book, who inspired this book and those yet to come in future projects. Once again, you demonstrate that indeed Allah has raised us from a dead state to life. Your stories are beautiful and full of testimony of the Teachings of the Most Honorable Elijah Muhammad. Finally, I want to thank Nisa Islam Muhammad, a true sister and professional whose efforts greatly assisted me with fulfilling the mission of service to the M.G.T. and G.C.C. and the Nation of Islam.

FOREWORD

Profiles in Courage provides an introduction to some of the most intriguing women — the women of the Nation of Islam. This book offers a look at the lives and loves of some of the women enrolled in the Muslim Girls Training and General Civilization Class (M.G.T. and G.C.C.). The class that shapes and molds women in the Nation of Islam is affectionately known as the MGT class and its students known as MGT. In most ways, they are just like other Muslim women. They bear witness that there is no God but Allah and Muhammad is His Messenger. They pray five times a day, fast during the Holy month of Ramadan, they give Zakat (charity) and when possible they make Hajj (pilgrimage to Mecca). Those five pillars unify Muslim women around the world from Indonesia to Iran to France and Canada.

The MGT however have undertaken a specific course of study that was designed to elevate the Black woman in America, many at the time of its inception in the 1930's and even today continued to exhibit the destructive vestiges of slavery. Allah intervened in their lives, in the affairs of Black people, in the person of Master Fard Muhammad. In 1930, he brought a course of study that he gave to his star student, the Most Honorable Elijah Muhammad. That study required that he read 104 books, most of which were about the life and Sunnah of the Prophet Muhammad, peace and blessings be upon him. The best of the 104 books according to the Honorable Elijah Muhammad was The Quran which he can be seen holding in numerous photos.

The women at the time were also given a weekly course of study in Islam that guides every aspect of her life. It is where she learns how Muslim women keep house, rear her children, care for her husband, sew, cook and in general how to act at home and abroad. In a modern world with out of wedlock childbirths near the same levels during slavery, the lowest marriage rates in the world, high divorce rates, increasingly poor health, a widening education achievement gap and more of the worst statistics of well-being in America, the

MGT Class rescues Black women from a degenerating society and gives her the tools to be successful as a civilized Muslim woman, wife and mother that is second to none.

Profiles in Courage introduces the reader to a variety of these women from all walks of life. Read about our doctors, lawyers, educators and more. Read about the women who have allowed Islam to change the status, stature and sanctity of the Black woman from the debilitating consequences of white supremacy, western ideologies and place her in a status second to none. Read about the women who teach, learn and shape a new future for themselves, their families and communities that impacts the U.S. and global landscape-both seen and unseen, socially, culturally, politically, and economically, today. Read about our Profiles in Courage.

Nisa I. Muhammad

In Health
Dr. Safiyya Shabazz
Dr. Stacey Muhammad
Odetta Muhammad
Dr. Mayyada Muhammad
Dr. Tisa Muhammad
Dr. Monique Muhammad

In Education
Lateefah Muhammad
Marva Muhammad
Majidah Muhammad
Dr. Cynthia McQueen Muhammad
Dr. Kathy Makeda Muhammad

In Arts & Culture
Kamora Muhammad
Faatimah Heaven Muhammad
Queen YoNasDa
Shernette Muhammad

In Justice/Defense
Sadiyah Evangelista X
Hassane Muhammad
Khaleelah Muhammad

In Agriculture/Science
Ann Mu'min Muhammad
Deborah Muhammad

In Information
Audrey Muhammad
Charlene Muhammad
Ebony Muhammad

In Spiritual Development
Ati Hamed Cushmeer
Ruth Muhammad
Nayyirah Tivicia Muhammad

IN HEALTH

From All
Walks of Life!

DR. SAFIYYA SHABAZZ
FAMILY MEDICINE DOCTOR/HUMANITARIAN SCHOLAR/WIFE & MOTHER

Safiyya Shabazz, MD, FAAFP is the owner and Medical Director of Fountain Medical Associates, PC. A graduate of Central High School of Philadelphia, she received her Bachelor of Science in Engineering and Medical Doctorate from the University of Pennsylvania. Dr. Shabazz is a recipient of the Melvin Molstad Prize in Chemical Engineering and the Nikitas J. Zervanos prize in Family Medicine.

She completed residency training at the University of Pennsylvania's Department of Family Medicine & Community Health where she previously served as a faculty member and remains on the volunteer faculty as an attending preceptor for Penn Med students. Dr. Shabazz is a diplomate of the American Board of Family Medicine and fellow of the American Academy of Family Physicians.

She lives in the Mount Airy section of Philadelphia with her husband and two children.

http://www.fountainmedonline.com/

DR. STACEY MUHAMMAD
MEDICAL DOCTOR/PALLIATIVE SPECIALIST
WIFE & MOTHER

Dr. Stacey Muhammad is a native Houstonian and the youngest of eight children. She graduated valedictorian in 1990 from Jack Yates High School. In high school she decided that she wanted to become a doctor. Dr. Muhammad attended the University of Texas at Austin, where she received her Bachelor's degree in Sociology/Pre- Med in 1995, and went on to attend the University of Texas- Houston Medical School in 1999 in the world- renowned Texas Medical Center.

She completed her residency training and became board-certified in Family Medicine, and started her own family practice in 2002, which she named the Abundant Life Clinic (of Houston). Dr. Muhammad was drawn to Hospice & Palliative Medicine, where she could manage pain and other symptoms in acutely ill patients with life- threatening illnesses. She found it extremely gratifying to help these patients and their families who are often at their most vulnerable.

Dr. Muhammad decided to subspecialize in this emerging field, and became board- certified in 2008 as a Hospice and Palliative Medicine physician. She is currently the Medical Director of Palliative Medicine at Memorial Hermann Southeast Hospital in Houston, Texas. Dr. Muhammad lives in Missouri City, Texas, is happily married to Frank Muhammad, and they are raising their sons, Mustapha and Nasheed.

Stacey Muhammad, M.D.
sisdrm@aol.com

ODETTA MUHAMMAD
NURSE EXECUTIVE/HEALTH ADVOCATE/COMMUNITY SERVANT/DAUGHTER/MOTHER/SISTER

"Honor thy mother and father on the earth so that your days will be long on the earth."

I was born in Panama, Central America, the same place my beautiful parents were also born, raised and married, and both of Jamaican descent. I could never thank Allah enough for my parents. It is because of their high family values, culture, moral convictions, and service to humanity that I am who I am today.

Born three months before my due date on a hot December day, my mother recalls my fighting spirit to live. My first bed was literally a shoe box. Not because my parents could not afford a crib, but because of my size. As I got "bigger" I was then given the luxury space of a dresser drawer as my abuela, tia's, tio's (grandmother, aunts and uncles) and many family friends would gather in amazement at my size and my fighting spirit while dressing me up in clothes and bows that weighed more than I did. What I most recall about my childhood in Panama is the sugar cane fields, my big brothers protection, and a culture of family and friends that were always together. Whenever I go back home to Panama, there is always a sense of nostalgia.

My parents migrated to the United States to offer their then, two children, my older brother and myself, a better education and better living. With four sibling's total, my parents sent all four of us to Catholic school from first grade through twelfth grade and sent all of us to college. I graduated from Morris Brown College where I pledged Alpha Kappa Alpha Sorority Incorporated with a BSN in Nursing. My career in nursing has included service in ICU, Med-surg, Antepartum, Emergency Room, Advice Nurse, and currently as charge nurse for Ambulatory services. With sincere humility I am grateful to have been nominated and have won awards throughout the span of my career that has included Ambulatory Nurse of the Year and The UnitedHealth Care DAISY Award. Serving my fellow nurses, I represent the ambulatory nurses on a Nursing Executive Council that is the governing body that determines the policies and procedures for the hospital as pertaining to nurse practices. I take great honor as a Certified Tobacco Treatment Specialist offering Smoking Cessation to the patients at Grady hospital and in the community. I believe that being a nurse is synonymous with being a servant of God, and so what better assignment in life could a person ask for.

I would say that my greatest accomplishment in my life was the day I became a Muslim and accepted the teachings of The Most Honorable Elijah Muhammad. My continued journey under the leadership of The Honorable Minister Louis Farrakhan. From Catholicism, to my upbringing in the Methodist church; and to a personal exploration in Seven Day Adventist church, I believed that Islam was the answer for that which all of my life has been my deep passion to understand: God's words, the spirituality of man and the condition of Black people.

My college sweetheart gave me as a birthday gift "Message to the Black Man in America" and after hearing a student minister of the Nation of Islam describe the Black man as a lion in a cage, unaware of his power and true relationship with a living God, I suddenly realized that what I was seeking to understand throughout my life became crystal clear and as scripture says "my heart yearned no more." "Islam has given my life complete meaning." I had to learn that the process of being a true Muslim is an evolving process that does not occur overnight nor has a period of completion.

My daily foundation is built from my favorite surah that is found in the Holy Quran Chapter 2:128 and from the instructions found in our study guides "Self-Improvement: The Basis for Community Development."

My favorite motto comes from the words of Michael Jackson's famous song Man in the Mirror where he says "And no message could have been any clearer. If you want to make the world a better place take a look at yourself and make a change." I say make that change by having first a personal relationship with God. I say make a change by working out of your passions and what conditions in life has impacted your life. Make that change by offering your gifts and talents given to you by Allah. I say make that change with the most valuable word to me that can be acted upon: Make that change with LOVE.

DR. MAYYADA MUHAMMAD
MEDICAL RESIDENT
WIFE & MOTHER

Born and raised in Atlanta, Georgia, Dr. Mayyada attended Muhammad's Mosque No.15. Her interest in science and human anatomy led her to Albany State University where she studied Forensic Science. During her sophomore year of college, Mayyada received a full scholarship to the Latin American School of Medicine in Havana, Cuba.

One word could be used to describe Dr. Mayyada Muhammad...Resilient. The daughter of two hardworking believers in the Nation of Islam, Sister Sandra and Brother

Sylvester Muhammad; the value of family and nation building was instilled in her at an early age. Mayyada always knew Allah would use her to serve her nation but she never could have imagined where his road would lead her.

At the age of nine, her mother was diagnosed with Lupus and scleroderma which piqued her interest in medicine and ultimately lead Mayyada to pursue a career in medicine. While studying Forensic science at Albany State University, she learned about the Cuban Medical Scholarship program, featured in the Final Call Newspaper. Mayyada saw this as the perfect opportunity to study medicine, live abroad, and learn a second language. By Allah's grace, Mayyada was accepted into the Latin American School of Medicine where she would receive an excellent medical education but more importantly acquire the skills required to address the biological, psychological, and social determinants of health. Mayyada began her studies in March of 2006.

Shortly after beginning her studies, The Honorable Minister Louis Farrakhan visited the Medical school along with his delegation. Allah confirmed she was on the straight path when The Minister held her hand and told her she could do it, "just stay the course no matter how tough it gets." These words continued to inspire Mayyada for the next 6 years. In October of 2012, only 9 months from graduation, The Minister made another visit to the school and once again Mayyada knew this was no coincidence but a sign from Allah that she was doing his will.

Dr. Mayyada graduated from medical school in July of 2013. She is thankful for everyone who supported her during six years of medical school especially her family and the believers of Muhammad's Mosque No.15 in Atlanta Georgia. Since graduation, Mayyada has completed her medical board exams and is currently in the 2016 National Residency Match for Family Medicine. She is a wife, mother, and community advocate. She is a member of several associations including The National Medical Association, Doctors for Global Health, and the American college of Preventive Medicine.

Dr. Mayyada believes everyone has the right to quality healthcare and education. Mayyada serves on the executive board for the Justice or Else Movement (Ministry of Health) to educate the community on vaccine injuries. In the future, she wants to work along with other physicians in the nation to build the first of many Nation of Islam owned hospitals.

DR. TISA MUHAMMAD
DOCTOR OF NATURAL MEDICINE/HOMEOPATHIC MEDICINE/WOMB WELLNESS CONSULTANT

"Surely I put my trust in Allah, my Lord and your Lord. There is no living creature but He grasps it by its forelock. Surely my Lord is on the right path."

~Surah 11, ayah 56

On a warm Wednesday morning in August, I was birthed into the arms of Lennox and Joan Farrell, my parents, young immigrant professionals from the beautiful islands of Trinidad and Tobago. I was the second born and would be the only daughter of four children.

True to life, my first hours were met with a problem of sorts. My parents, seeking a name that was worthy enough for me, left me nameless as they searched through countless books for what would fit. A family friend, Mrs. Phipps, upon discovering their dilemma, encouraged them to christen me with, "Tisa." Not knowing the meaning, when they discovered its origin was in Kenya, my father, upon my enquiry always told me that my name, "means the number '9' in Kiswahili," and that was what I thought until I discovered its beautiful Arabic origin was the same. That was also my first introduction to the science of numbers, numbers that would continually be present in my life.

My earliest memories of childhood were grand. I remember traveling from a very young age on planes to the Caribbean, spending Winters splash dancing in warm sun showers, Summers at either of our Grandmothers' homes, with our big happy, rambunctious family; or taking sea baths in the inviting salt waters of the Atlantic Ocean, baths that in hindsight, seemed to last all day.

By the time I was seven years old, I was establishing myself as a public figure of sorts, following in my fathers' political activism, chanting down Babylon or motivating our Black Community in Toronto to rally against oppression- both near and as far away as South Africa and her apartheid system. My family was not only immediately those who were in my household or in the islands, Europe or America, but, I learned very early that my "family" extended to dozens of "Aunts," "Uncles," and "Cousins" from our closely knit Black Conscious community. I was thoroughly loved and nurtured on "blackness" and it was satisfying to my young soul~!

True to form, interestingly, the year that I turned nine- my joyous life took a uniquely pivotal turn- one that would truly define an aspect of my mission and life's journey. The first was when I heard the Adhan (Muslim call to prayer) and the Al Fatihah, the first chapter in the Quran, performed less than a foot away from my seat in one of our many "Community Town Hall" meetings. It was heartily sung by our family friend, an Imam, whom we all lovingly called "Brother Bilal". That event marked the moment that I chose to be a Muslim, as I noticed not only the peace felt in the words, but, among other things, the discipline our "Uncle Brother Bilal" exemplified. There were many more Muslims who peppered and seasoned this life decision, reinforcing something that was not present to me to the same extent in my own upbringing in Adventism.

The second indelible point in my life was defined by my first exposure to our suffering, when my father showed us a documentary about the savage murder of a young boy, lovingly called, "Emmett Till". This was my earliest memory of feeling the intense pain of injustice for our people.

Although, prior to this event I was taught about our suffering, even that personal ones of my own ancestors' struggles and triumphs- like my great-great Grandmother Titi who, being kidnapped and sold off the West African shores, jumped off of a slave ship hoping for death's awaiting arms, only to find enough life and the prospect of freedom to swim to the shores of Carriacou in the Grenadine Islands, northeast of the Island of Grenada; or, my Great-Great Grandmother, known to us as "Ma" who, upon hearing of the horrific disfiguring punishment of the women of the Congo, who, through the order of "The Butcher of the Congo," King Leopold II of Belgium, were having their breasts chopped off for not producing enough rubber for their Colonial masters, marched with thousands of other women in defiant protest of the atrocities.

Islam called me again. I was 17 years of age when I took shahadah and accepted the Teachings of the Most Honorable Elijah Muhammad, through the Honorable Min Louis Farrakhan.

My life as a Muslim was enhanced with trials and tribulations as well as the victories of growth and much needed self-development. Since I was so studied in the Bible, prior to accepting Islam, it was not hard for me to feel confident in the direction that the Minister was taking my young mind. I was no longer caught up in Nationalistic Political Activism, I saw the Human family as more than just the descendants of Africa, rather the Black man and woman were now the Original People.

The price I paid for the cause was great. I lost a lot of popularity on my school campus as I covered up my body in modesty and kept my natural hair under wraps and headpieces. By the time I graduated, I discovered that many students, upon leaving Oakwood, also joined the Nation of Islam because of our committed example. We were so resilient in our faith walk, enduring attacks- both verbal and in one case against my friend, Nkenge Muhammad, physical. We maintained our silence against the insults, continuing to stand up for what we believed. I will not pretend that it was not, at times, unnerving, but, despite it all, when we stayed prayerful, we were successful.

Lately, with over twenty years of being in this experience of being Muslim, I have discovered an insatiable desire to explore more about Allah, as seen through the study of the Sciences and Nature. It seems that no matter where I go, if I apply this Teaching, I can finally see Him present, even in, as they say the whispering of the winds, other religious faiths and their holy texts.

My attraction to the Nation of Islam was in the manner in which our women are treated. There are rarely any organizations that place the woman on a higher pedestal than that granted to us through the Teachings of the Most Hon Elijah Muhammad. "No Nation can rise any higher than its woman!" This phrase was so inscribed on my mind, when I first heard it, that I had no choice but to submit and find myself in the ranks.

One of my many favorite quotes from the Most Honorable Elijah Muhammad, are his words to the Honorable Minister Louis Farrakhan- "When you discover WHO you are, YOU WON'T be able to HOLD YOUR SELF DOWN!" To me, those words are the very keys to our own sacred journey in this Mission, as we determine to "Accept our own and be ourselves."

Currently, I have been inspired to spread Islam on a Global level, through my organization, A Phoenix Rising Wellness Institute (APRWI). As a Doctor of Natural Medicine, it is my desire to spread Islam to our family in the Caribbean, Africa and throughout the rest of the World.

In essence, it is my desire to be remembered as being "The Qur'an Walking". Just like Prophet Muhammad (Peace and blessings be upon him), and the exemplary walk of the Minister, The Messenger and the examples given for our consideration by Master Fard Muhammad.

I am a mother of seven children and I have a Doctor of Natural Medicine/Homeopathic Medicine with a B.S. in Orthomolecular Medicine and an A.S. in Physical Therapy. I am Certified as a Clinical Iridologist and a Certified Holistic Healthcare Consultant. Most recently I was trained in the NADA technique in Acupuncture. I am a Womb Worker, a Womb Wellness Consultant and a Womb Warrior- working daily to heal myself in order to assist other women with keeping and healing their wombs, as collectively, we heal our families, our communities, our world and ultimately this beautiful Planet Earth.

DR. MONIQUE MUHAMMAD
PSYCHOLOGIST/EDUCATOR/ COMMUNITY SERV-
ANT/ENTREPRENEUR/ WIFE & MOTHER

Dr. Monique Muhammad was introduced to the Nation of Islam through a Final Call Newspaper given to her in the mid-80s. That paper planted a seed that was later watered in 1987, at a time when some considered her a "pro-black, radical" college student at Rutgers University. A fellow student (now FOI) showed her a videotape of the Honorable Minister Louis Farrakhan. The Minister was speaking about separation and presented the absolute most tenable lecture that she had ever heard. This same brother arranged for a van ride to Muhammad Mosque #80 in Plainfield, New Jersey that Sunday where Minister Kareem

Muhammad was talking about building a black army. Without reservation or hesitation, she made an immediate commitment to become a Muslim and work on the mission of the Nation of Islam. Over two decades later, she is still actively involved in and committed to the Nation of Islam.

Dr. Monique began her professional career, immediately after graduating from college, as a counselor in a school-based drug prevention program. As she continued to pursue varied work experiences, she also continued to pursue her education. She later earned a Master of Arts degree in Counseling and ultimately went on to earn her doctoral degree in Psychology.

Dr. Muhammad currently runs her own private practice in Woodbridge, New Jersey as a general practitioner, who treats a wide range of mental illnesses in adolescents and adults. She, however, specializes in, and is most passionate about, marriage counseling. In addition to her clinical work, Dr. Monique also does Work-life Balance/ Wellness presentations for client companies of ComPsych Corporation, on a consultant basis. She also develops and delivers presentations for private requestors as well. Volunteer service is also a significant part of her repertoire of professional activity. Dr. Monique serves on the executive board of the New Jersey Chapter of the Association of Black Psychologists and is a volunteer board member for her county's Juvenile Conference Committee and Child Placement

Review Board. Dr. Monique feels blessed because she loves her work and believes that through her work as a helping professional, she has found her purpose.

She is the proud mother of three very talented and intelligent registered MGT. Her eldest daughter Atiya Muhammad (21 years old) is currently teaching high school in Baltimore, Maryland. Dr. Monique recently delighted in visiting and observing Atiya's classes in the days approaching 10.10.15 and engaging with her students about Justice or Else and other related topics.

Her second daughter Ayanna Muhammad is currently a Junior in a Pre-Medicine program at Seton Hall University, with an interest in holistic health. She fondly recalls how

Ayanna taught her about GMOs way before it became a well-known and popular topic of interest.

Her youngest daughter, Qadirah Muhammad (17 years old), is currently in her Freshman year at Rutgers University. Dr. Monique treasures Qadirah's determination, drive, and boldness. Qadirah embodies the saying, "You can do whatever you put your mind to."

For Dr. Monique, her nine-year marriage to Majied Muhammad is also an integral part of who she is. Through her marriage, she is beginning to know completeness and balance from a spiritual perspective. She reveres that as Allah has blessed Majied to be the man that he is, she is finally safe to become who Allah wants her to be.

Allah-u-Akbar

IN EDUCATION

When you teach a man, you teach an individual, but when you teach a woman, you teach a nation!

LATEEFAH MUHAMMAD
EDUCATOR/ WIDOW/ MOTHER
BREAST CANCER WARRIOR

Bismillah. As-Salaam Alaikum.

By Allah's Grace, I have been blessed to be a Muslim and student of Teachings of the Most Honorable Elijah Muhammad under the leadership of the Honorable Minister Louis Farrakhan for over thirty years. I am a Registered Member of the Nation of Islam and a Sister of The Muslim Girls' Training and General Civilization Class of Muhammad Mosque No. 24 in Richmond, Virginia.

Among my most amazing experiences are having the honor to serve as the Student Trainer of Women and Girls in the MGT and GCC for Muhammad Mosque No. 38 and a very brief but rewarding tenure in Norfolk, VA. Also to have been among those to serve the Honorable Minister Louis Farrakhan as a member of the awesome Torchlight Cooking and Serving Team of the Mid-Atlantic Region.

In the field of my passion, education, I currently serve as an online Instructor of Language Arts for Muhammad Universities of Islam No. 4 (Washington, DC) and 24. As a Registered Behavioral Technician, I work with Autistic and Special Needs children providing in-home therapy and assistance. For the past nine years, in the summers, I have served as Director for the Walker-Grant Alumni Association Summer Education program. It supports children with behavioral challenges by developing education, social and cultural plans to enrich their lives, designing and providing an academic, arts and cultural program.

Fulfilling the dream to be able to teach Black youth with truth and authenticity, I was blessed to be an original teacher of Muhammad University of Islam No. 4 in

Washington, DC and to eventually serve as its Director and Regional Director of Education. When faxing was the mode of communication, I was blessed to work with parents in Richmond, VA to establish what we now call "Distance Learning."

Hampton University is where I earned my Bachelor's degree, and extended my education with matriculation at George Mason University, University of Mary Washington College, the University of Virginia, and most recently enrolled and completed a Course in the online School of Supreme Wisdom- Curriculum Development founded by Sister Deborah Muhammad (Baton Rouge, LA). I have also taken drafting and architecture classes at the local community college.

Additionally, I taught art for ten years in public education. I returned to the University of Mary Washington (UMW) College as a counselor in the Student Transition Program, where working with Black students to assist in their successful transition from small rural communities to life on a large predominantly white campus. I was an original instructor for the renowned James Farmer Scholar Program at UMW. Wanting to work in the community, I established NAJM Academy/ Muhammad University of Islam Learning Center in 1994 and continue to operate the education consulting firm. It serves educators, parents and students through professional training and development workshops, skills courses, evaluations and assessments, online education, tutoring; and through NAJM Academy, I partner with local organizations to design and implement community education programs. Under the same name I owned and operated a private day school in Columbia, SC.

As a 40 plus year educator, I taught in the Charlottesville, Stafford County and Fredericksburg school systems in Virginia. In Fredericksburg, I established the STARS (Students Taking Alternative Resources for Success) Program, a successful alternative education program that remains in operation today. Most recently, I served as the Director of Education at Blake Farm Day School in Fredericksburg for the past eight years. My recent speaking engagements include the 2013 NAACP (Richmond) Education Conference; 100 Black Men of Central Virginia M-Cube Education Conference, and Shiloh Baptist Church Health and Wellness

Counsel in 2014. I also served as a panelist and radio presenter for 10-10-15 Justice or Else! From time to time, I am asked by the Final Call Newspaper for perspectives on education. My art background keeps me as a long-time member of the Harambee 360 Degrees Cultural Arts program of Fredericksburg, exhibiting my original art bi-annually at the local arts festival.

I have home schooled my seventeen year old son, and I have an adult daughter and grandson. I enjoy family and friends, being a Sister/Sistah, student, servant, daughter, mother, homemaker, artist, and educator. This is my thirteenth year as a Breast Cancer Warrior; widow of a wonderful fallen FOI (may Allah be pleased with him). I love being in nature and spend as much time as I can camping and even climbing area mountains. I love being…

Marva Y. Muhammad

Educator/Teacher/Seamstress
Daughter/Mother/Sister

I am the second daughter of, Eli Michael Baker, and Vera Ruth McFarland Baker, both deceased. I was born in Los Angeles, California. My mother was an administrative assistant for Kaiser Hospital and my father was a quality control inspector for Lockheed Martin Aircraft. When I was born, they had been divorced for quite some time, so having them in the same household was never the case for me and my sister. This also meant that I had the opportunity to spend time with both and I never missed having one in my early childhood.

When I was four, my mother moved us to a small town in northern California, Pacific Grove. It is, to me, one of the most beautiful communities I have ever lived in. Although the population of Black people at that time was small, I never felt I was missing out on anything from my own community. My mother was a strong proponent of "Blackness" and would never let us forget who we were. As a matter of fact, the only Black church, in the town, Missionary Baptist Church, was where we regularly attended. My mother was more spiritual than religious. She never forced us to believe, she just considered our Sunday routine, more exposure than indoctrination. She taught me how to read the Bible, and would read to me from it as my bedtime story. She taught me how to pray. And she gave me a strong since of understanding that God is the only reality.

My mother passed away in 1986; after a long battle with lung cancer. As you can imagine that was the worst type of motivation. But I was motivated. When she died, I promised to be the best and to do my best to complete college and make her proud. I moved to Monroe, Louisiana, and lived with my granduncle and aunt, Joe and Barbara Davis. I finished high school at Carroll High in Monroe, Louisiana.

In 1987, I started my college career at Florida A&M University and spent a year and half there. I transferred back to Louisiana, and entered Grambling State University. I received my Bachelor of Arts degree in Mass Communications and Public Relations. I also thought I wanted to be a photo journalist before pursuing a teaching degree. Ironically, the week before graduation, I vowed that I would go back and get my teaching degree, immediately.

In 2004, I graduated from the University of Louisiana at Monroe. I received a Masters Degree in Teaching in Special Education. I taught at Berg Jones Elementary school for three years. In 2007, I received a general education endorsement, and moved to Cypress Point University Elementary School, where I taught for eleven years.

When I was 15 years old I saw, the Honorable Louis Farrakhan on a news broadcast. Jesse Jackson was a candidate in the 1984 Presidential campaign. I was fascinated by the way he spoke. That was the first time I had ever seen Black Muslims. A few years later while visiting my father, I purchased a copy of the Message to the Blackman. I read it, but did not really understand it. A close friend invited me to the local study group in Monroe, after our discussion of both the Honorable Elijah Muhammad and Min. Farrakhan. I attended that meeting, and saw the MGT for the first time. I felt like I had come home. I started the process to join the Nation of Islam at the end of 1993 in Monroe, and completed it in 1994, after my return to Los Angeles.

What has Islam done for me? It is the question we ask another believer, as a way of giving our testimonials. It is our way of spreading the word of truth about what life experience that changed or saved a "wretch" like me. My testimony about why I chose this way of life is simple. I did not choose Islam, it chose me. I started asking those important questions, like "who is God", "if Adam and Eve had two sons, where did the rest of the people come from?" I did not get the answers at church, simply because they were not there. The more I questioned the more Islam as taught by the Honorable Elijah Muhammad and his *best* student, the Honorable Louis Farrakhan, answered. I also know that through all the trials of life that my faith and deep desire to persevere has been my saving grace. This teaching is not for the faint of heart, it is for those who desire to know *God* and to know *self.*

In 2002, my daughter was diagnosed with Wilm's Tumor, a childhood kidney cancer. To some that may have been a lot. But I know that I was prepared for that war. My early life experiences made me prepared and my present spiritual path made me battle ready. And fight, we did. We survived to tell the story and it is only by the grace and mercy of Allah.

I am currently attending Walden University pursuing my Doctoral degree in Education. I am writing a book for parents of young children with cancer, and I, of course, am doing what I love, teaching.

MAJIDAH MUHAMMAD
EDUCATOR/WIFE & MOTHER

Majidah Muhammad, a second generation Muslim, is currently a Domestic Engineer in Chicago, IL. with her husband Khabir and son Haqq. After graduating from Spelman College, Magna Cum Laude, with a B.A. in Child Development, she joined Teach for America in 2009 and began teaching Pre-K in the DC Public School System. In 2011, she graduated from George Mason University with an M.A. in Curriculum and Instruction. Her love for children and education kept her in the classroom for six years.

During that time, her commitment to providing the best education for her class found her picking up students who were chronically late to school, washing the hair of students coming from challenging home lives, visiting parents to teach them how to teach their children and providing countless hours of additional teaching to her students to ensure their success.

Teaching was just the beginning for her. The classroom experience and what she brought to it as well as what she received from it has pre-pared Majidah to advocate for change over the course of her life, as an educator and parent.

She is a life-long learner and enjoys traveling. She realizes that whatever a person cares most about - our economy, education, fashion, health care, scientific theology, our community - a great education is at the heart of changing things for the better. She hopes to continue to be a cata-lyst for change. Majidah Muhammad is currently working on a series of Muslim children's books.

DR. CYNTHIA McQUEEN MUHAMMAD
EDUCATOR, TORCHLIGHT ACADEMY
WIFE & MOTHER

Dr. Cynthia Muhammad, an author, has served as a Super-intendent, Principal, College Professor, Vice Principal, Guidance Counselor, and teacher. She has a bachelor's degree, master's degree, and a Doctorate.   Dr. Cynthia is also a former television show host, radio talk show host, radio announcer and newspaper reporter.

She has been nominated for the following awards: Out-standing Young Women of America, Dynamic Women We Admire, Educator of the Year and Black Marriage

Day: Couple of the Year. She has also been featured in Virtue Magazine Outstanding Women Issue and Spectacular Magazine's Woman of the Year issue.

In 2014, Dr. Cynthia was nominated to become a member of the State Board of Education.

She has been married to her college sweetheart for over 40 years. Together they have two successful adult children and three beautiful grandchildren.

Dr. Kathy Makeda Muhammad
EDUCATOR/HUMANITARIAN
SCHOLAR/WIFE & MOTHER

Dr. Kathy Makeda Muhammad was born in Winston-Salem, North Carolina and grew up in the Morningside Community. She graduated from Parkland High School in 1978. Dr. Muhammad attended Shaw University and graduated Summa Cum Laude in 2001 with a B.A. in Sociology. While attending Shaw she received the following scholarships and awards:

Who's Who Among Students in American Universities & Colleges, 2000-2001
William R. Hearst Scholar, 1999-2000
Shaw University Academic Achievement Award – Gold Metal, 1999-2000
Shaw University Academic Achievement Award – Pinnacle Award, 1999-2000

Member, Alpha Chi Honor Society, Inducted 1999
The National Dean's List, 1998-1999, Undergraduate Studies

In 2001, Dr. Muhammad became an East Tennessee State University Ronald McNair Research Scholar. Upon completing 208 hours of research on a "welfare-to-work" program, she applied to Union Institute & University and was accepted. In 2009, Dr. Muhammad received a PhD in African Women's/Black Studies from Union Institute & University. While attending UI&U she received the following scholarships and awards:

Union Institute & University Graduate Scholarship, 2007
Daniel J. Ransohoff Scholarship, 2007
National Dean's List, 2007-2008, Graduate Studies

Dr. Muhammad is the mother of two children and grandmother of five. She has two siblings and is an aunt of several nieces and nephews. Dr. Muhammad is an educator of Black History and Pan Africanism, an independent researcher and chess player. She is founder and director of AlkebuLearning Foundation, which is based in Accra. The objectives of her foundation are:

(1) To help promote mutual understanding and knowledge between Black people throughout the diaspora and those on the continent of Africa: (2) To assist in providing a "rites of passage" for youth from different cultural, religious and spiritual affiliations and national groups: and (3) To help improve the conditions of the people by striving to provide educational materials and resources.

She repatriated to Africa in 2011 and resides in Ghana. Dr. Muhammad's determined spirited was nurtured by her loving parents the late James M. Bailey Jr. and Martha Tucker-Bailey: her willingness to finish her collegiate education was encouraged by her supportive and caring mentors, the late Drs. Lorenzo Battle III and Josephine Bradley and inspiration to continue forward, regardless of adversity from the Honorable Minister Louis Farrakhan, Mother Tynnetta Muhammad and Attorney Sister Ava Muhammad.

Photo Courtesy of Hasan Muhammad

"We must respect and honor women if the nation is ever to be great. When we do not have a proper appreciation for women, this is reflected in women's roles in the society. Women should be active in every field of endeavor except those that degrade them.

Why is it that a woman who is exceedingly beautiful must model filth and indecency? Why can't she model something beautiful and righteous instead of being a saleswoman for filth? Why is it that if she is a singer we end up seeing more of her bosom than hearing her voice? The righteous are sick of the degradation of women. The maintenance of women as sex objects is destroying the society."

—Minister Louis Farrakhan
Twitter, Published Friday, January 17, 2014 at 4:50pm.

IN ARTS & CULTURE

Civilization is Never Measured by its Men, It is Measured by its Women!

KAMORA MUHAMMAD
SKILLED SEAMSTRESS/ TEACHER/ DOULA, NANNY/ SISTER/ WIFE/ MOTHER

Kamora Muhammad, was born and raised in Dallas, Texas. She is a proud member of Muhammad Mosque No. 48 in Dallas where she currently serves as First Officer of the M.G.T. and G.C.C. By the grace of almighty God, Allah, she received her "X" in 1994 in New Orleans, Louisiana as a college student while attending Muhammad Mosque No. 46 where the late Harold Muhammad was the minister. She is one of two children and was raised by her grand-parents and aunts who made sure she was well traveled throughout her childhood. They also instilled a love of God, self and black people in her as well. Her mother taught her to love her skin. Her father taught her that there is strength and power in silence. Allah has blessed her with a wonderful husband of 20 years, Robert Muhammad, who is her biggest supporter in so many ways. They have a beautiful daughter, Qiyamah Muhammad, who is growing up to be a soldier in Muhammad's Vanguard while in college. Kamora is so grateful for the village that raised and molded her life. It truly does take a village to raise a child.

Allah has blessed her with so many positive influences that will forever impact her. As a high school student her favorite teacher, Juanita Simmons, took her along with a group of students to Africa. This trip changed her life. She later followed in Mrs. Simmons footsteps and took the students of Muhammad University of Islam of Dallas to Africa in 2006 where she served as teacher for fifteen years and director for five of those years. That same teacher introduced her to the Honorable Minister Louis Farrakhan via a television show. Kamora knew at that moment she wanted to be with this powerful and uncompromising black man. She has been studying Islam and following the teachings of the Most Honorable Elijah Muhammad under the leadership of Minister Farrakhan ever since. Under his divine leadership, she is learning to understand the value of being a good Muslim.

With Allah's help, she taught herself how to sew. Since she is somewhat of a perfectionist, she got it right the first time, zipper and all. It turns out that her maternal grand-mother was a professional seamstress. So, it is in her D.N.A. She attributes this to her natural ability to sew. Her former M.G.T. Captain, Sis. Vickie Muhammad, who is a phenomenal seamstress would share sewing tips and she would take heed without hesitation. She also encouraged her to teach others to sew and to sew for others. She began to do so shortly after. She now sews for her husband, women and children all over the nation. She loves to see her clothes on the sisters and often thinks who knew that she would be making clothes at all. Allah is the Best Knower.

When Kamora is not sewing, she is quite busy. Serving the believers brings her great joy. Spending time with her family is her favorite interest. Planning and organizing for mosque related events is often part of her duties that she loves. She has passion for studying anything related to health and healing. To relieve stress, she likes to Crossfit, lift weights, box, train in martial arts, cycle, and run. One of her happiest moments was finishing her first marathon after months of training. Incorporating the training units into daily living is of utmost importance.

With the help of Allah, Kamora desires to grow her sewing business which is called Truly Your's Modest Fashions and hire other sisters to work with her.

http://www.trulyyoursmodestfashions.com/

FAATIMAH MUHAMMAD
FASHION & MODELING
COLLEGE STUDENT, MAJOR, NURSING

Faatimah Muhammad was born Muslim in New York City in The Nation of Islam, under the leadership of The Honorable Minister Louis Farrakhan. Faatimah came from a family of professionals who had careers in many aspects of healthcare. At the tender age of 11 years old, she developed a natural, keen eye for fashion, which was just thought to be something young girls go through. What they did not know was that fashion would become something that would serve as a major significance in her later life. Through her development and training in The Nation of Islam, at a young age, Faatimah had a strong will to serve her nation and people through her skills, knowledge and talents, and promote The Nation of Islam's culture. This was her personal mission.

During her summer breaks from George Washington Carver High School, where she attended as a science major, Faatimah applied to Queens General Hospital for their annual summer youth employment. Faatimah worked for three consecutive summers, in the pediatric department, Radiology department and Cancer center. This gave her the motivation to continue with her studies, as well as the hands-on experience, giving her a glimpse into what she would be pursuing in her later life.

After graduating from George Washington Carver High School, Faatimah attended college, where she pursued her studies in Nursing. Faatimah applied for her first healthcare related job at Atria Senior Living facility, where she cared for the geriatrics community. Wanting to dive further into the healthcare realms, Faatimah later applied to one of the top magnet, hospitals in the city, which is a very challenging hospital to get into. Faatimah impressed the entire board with her upbeat, youthful professionalism, articulation, and knowledge, (that she credits to her training that she received from The Nation of Islam), that they did not need to interview her a second time. She received an email a few days later congratulating her on her hire. There she became a part of the Nurs-

ing Department team, serving as a member on the float pool, where she provides healthcare in the majority of the hospital's units/departments.

Besides her career in the nursing field, Faatimah began to pursue modeling as a way to fulfill her interest in the world of fashion. Faatimah earned various modeling gigs; which consisted of both runway, as well as print work. Keeping her dress code standards at the forefront, Faatimah was very hands-on and worked with the designers, and stylists so that she could be certain that she would be respecting herself and the nation through her representations on the runway, while still respecting and embracing the creative genius of the designer's craft. Many designers were creative and open to the new fashion ideas and expressions she introduced, that they made certain changes for her.

Faatimah's first modeling gig was through Jennifer Muhammad who is a fashion designer from Chicago, Illinois, who designs clothes catering to, but not limited to, The Nation of Islam. With Faatimah's many experiences, she saw a power within modeling that she could use to usher in modesty as a refreshing, urban style trend. Keeping her mission on hand, Faatimah decided to take modeling seriously. She saw that her knowledge and experience of fashion could help to influence the minds of those in the fashion industry, so that fashion, which is used today sometimes as a weapon against women, to sexualize and exploit them, could be used as a tool to respectfully glorify them. Faatimah's personal sense of style, natural keen eye for fashion and creativity was noticed and quickly earned her major tasks by designers and others. She has worked with creative directors, stylists, fashion consultants, and production coordinators, just to name a few. Faatimah has modeled for "Exclusive Designs Inc", "Bobiar Designs", "Brownstone," "Fashon", "Newworld Apparel", "Traveling Pillar" "Motives Cosmetics"etc. She earned a 5 page spread in "Virtue Magazine," and later returned, gracing the cover of the international edition ("Justice or Else") of "Virtue magazine." She also earned an interview in "Heal Thy Life" magazine.

Through her continued growing exposure and knowledge in the industry, Faatimah has used her ability to style women by helping them express themselves through fashion, while encouraging them to maintain their body mystic. Faatimah has styled women from their own closets, and has assisted in their personal shopping to advise them in taking a modest approach, while remaining current to the trends.

Faatimah has offered a glimpse into her world of styling through the use of social media. On her Instagram and Facebook, she has displayed some of her seasonal styles from her own personal wardrobe, as a way to reach the masses of women, from all over, and offer a message of raising the bar through their presentation of themselves to the world. Through her works, she continues to reach and achieve her goals of inspiring many women from all walks of life, all ages, races, cultures, and faiths. Faatimah has received many words of gratitude for her continued efforts, in helping to redefine the image of women, from the world's perspective, through fashion.

PHOTOS OF FAATIMAH BY: SAAJIDA MUHAMMAD (NYC)

She's Not Heavy! She's My Sister!

Photo Courtesy of Aiwal Toure/Elton Muhammad

QUEEN YONASDA *pronounced Yo-Naja-Ha*
COMMUNITY ACTIVIST & ORGANIZER
MUSIC ARTIST/DAUGHTER/MOTHER

Peace and Blessings, my name is YoNasDa (Queen Yo-NasDa) pronounced Yo-Naja-Ha. I am a proud Oglala Lakota and Black woman. I am the National Director of the Indigenous Nations Alliance-Millions More Movement. I am also a published writer & Hip Hop Artist.

"No Nation Can Rise Higher Than It's Woman," is a saying that breathes truth. Queen YoNasDa epitomizes this energy as a hip hop artist, curator, and activist. Without a doubt, there is an imbalance occurring in hip hop where female emcees have been silenced. Her strong presence is bringing femcees with a message back to the forefront of music as the days of Queen Latifah and Lauryn Hill with a modern twist. Her musical style encompasses an eclectic mix of wisdom, grooves, catchy hooks, and is sure to reach the masses.

Queen YoNasDa entered the music industry by choreographing for BET's Teen Summit, Planet Groove and Soundstage. She opened nationally on the Wu Tang Clan 8 Diagrams Tour (Winter 2008-2009). Along the way she has performed with many other artists from Lloyd, Ginuwine, Method Man & Redman, Jurassic 5, Christina Aguilera & Many more. She has appeared on various mixtapes and albums (Flip Ya Wigs Compilation, Kanye West presents Malik Yusef "G.O.O.D Morning-G.O.O.D Night" 2009, 2006 Wu South Mixtape, 2006) & artists albums Cappadonna "The Transition," Shaka Amazulu the 7th – Debut (UK artist), Atllas "Hunger & Starvation", and completing her own debut album God, Love & Music (Released October 2009). Also look for her single Pow Wow" in the Empire Films movie "Diamond Dawgs: Code 487".

Queen YoNasDa just completed her first national co-headlining tour with Wu Tang Clan's Raekwon alongside Capone N Noreaga "Built For Cuban Linx 2 Tour" (Nov.13-Dec 19, 2009). She performed songs from her highly respected album "God. Love & Music" that hit retail/digital stores internationally October 27, 2009. She also released her follow up single "So Special" produced by Grammy award winning producer No ID.

"I'm not here to beat people in the head with a sermon, I'm here to tell the truth," she explains. This lyrical queen released her debut album independently with Kingz N Queenz/101 Distribution, "God, Love and Music" featuring Cappadonna, Dr. Ben Chavis Muhammad, Keith Murray, M-Eighty and others with production by Cookin Soul, New York West, CR Productions, K-Boog and others. She speaks and performs across the United States promoting unity, education and respect for all cultures.

As a young child, YoNasDa stood by her mother's and grandfather's, (Minister Louis Farrakhan), side speaking to the hip hop nation. She remembered when he uttered "one of a rapper's songs is equivalent to five of his speeches." As an emcee, YoNasDa is living proof. She takes her responsibility seriously by using her music as a mouth piece to educate and uplift young people. As a mother, she sees what music can do and understands the power of the spoken word.

YoNasDa has a mission and is going full throttle. She is the national director for the Indigenous Nations Alliance-Millions More Movement. She spearheaded a 32 city fundraising event called Hip Hop 4 Haiti, as well as mobilized Arizona's rappers with the permission of Public Enemy to remake "By The Time I Get to Arizona-Back 2 AZ (Anti-SB1070). This truth-teller is a published writer who has a weekly column in the Final Call Newspaper and is now bringing her artistry to the world. Queen YoNasDa is the estranged wife of Wu Tang Clan's Cappadonna and a mother of two sons. To YoNasDa "Queen" is not just a word, it is a calling and she's rising to the occasion.

At 10.10.15 Justice or Else. Photo Courtesy of Kay Lawal-Muhammad

www.queenyonasda.com www.kingznqueenzllc.com

SHERNETT MUHAMMAD
ACCLAIMED ARTISIT/ NATION OF ISLAM PAINTER
TEACHER/ PERFORMING ART CHOREOGRAPHER

Visual Artist Shernett Muhammad was born in Saint Andrews, Jamaica and moved to the United States in the early 80's. She graduated from the Art Institute of Fort Lauderdale with an Associates of Science degree in Fashion Illustration. Shernett is a self-taught artist and around age 12, discovered a real passion for drawing. She has developed this innate talent into detailed renditions of the beauty of humanity and nature.

Shernett perceives *"Life* as a moving canvas; a Living Work of Art and were all masterpieces of the Creator are on display in Life's Gallery." Hence, her thematic paintings are inspired by life events. They are visual stories, snapshots of the Creator's Genius and Artistry we see in the Art of Creation.

"Everything is art!" From this realization, Shernett draws inspiration from things and people she sees in her day to day travels. While these things may not be so interesting to others she sees them as outstanding. Inspiration is never hard to find, Shernett says, "As soon as I complete one painting that feeling of satisfaction fills me and I begin to scan the landscape and horizon for a new high, a new subject to capture that feeling again, therefore, I do not have to search for inspiration, it's all around me."

Her primary medium used in creating works of art are acrylic paints on canvas and wood. She finds acrylics to be more pliable and brilliant in color, application and in its final result. Other mediums she uses are oil paints, pastels, watercolors, colored pencils and graphite pencils. She also uses a camera to capture her subject and the finer more intricate details her eyes alone would nullify shortly thereafter.

Shernett became a Muslim in the Nation of Islam on June 8, 1994 and says, "It is by far the most fulfilling and promising experience of her life to-date." The Nation of Islam, the study, culture and way of life that we strive to live up to never fails to evolve me mentally, spiritually and physically.

That said, Shernett states, "We have an extraordinary Nation and blooming culture that is coming to birth in the world. History must not find the names of others to be more prevalent than the names of members of the Nation of Islam documenting and telling our story through the arts and sciences. Others will not do us justice in telling our history; those who do not see us properly or understand who we are in past, present or future should not be the more outspoken or more visible on documenting or representing our culture and history in any form. As visual and performing artists, writers and authors, doctors, engineers, and educators, whatever field of endeavor we are engaged in, we must tell our history, traditions and cultural sojourn and evolution in the Nation of Islam and representing it well! Or someone else will do it for us and we may not be so pleased with their depiction of us.

This painting is titled "A Culture of Learning." The pleasantly, radiant women are depicted in this tranquil café setting engrossed in study and dialogue. They are students of the Muslim Girls Training and General Civilization Class of the Nation of Islam (M.G.T. & G.C.C.). Besieged and absorbed by literature; their expressions reveal astuteness, insightfulness, contentment, and an eagerness for knowledge. The women in the painting portray the fundamental culture of the Nation of Islam, "A Culture of Learning," which upholds a commitment to one's self in the pursuit of knowledge for the advancement of self, family, nation, and humanity in accordance with the will of Allah.

The next painting came about as a request by our National Student Captain Sister Sandy Muhammad. She desired to give Mother Khadijah Farrakhan a gift from and on behalf of the women of the Nation of Islam, The M.G.T. and G.C.C.

Once again, the painting is a depiction of one of the most important aspects of the culture of the women and girls in the Nation of Islam. This painting titled, "Seeded Minds: Year of the Farm" captures and shows the energy and environment at that time; wherein, the women were engrossed in an intense study and dialogue based on the lessons and teachings of the Hon. Elijah Muhammad and an introduction to and study of Dianetics, The Modern Science of Mental Health, which, the Honorable Minister Louis Farrakhan strategically placed the students of the N.O.I. on this course study.

The Title "Seeded Minds: Year of the Farm" came about on two separate occasions; one wherein, the Minister had placed the MGT on this intense study and two, in a Tuesday night lecture that same year wherein, he stated, this year would be called, "The Year of the Farm." The two correlated to me, in both instance, the Minister was tilling, cultivating and planting seeds of knowledge and wisdom in the mind of the women and girls of the MGT as much as he was tilling, cultivating and planting physical seeds in the earth at the farm for both our physical nourishment and economic growth and development of us as a people.

We must be the minds and hands to write our history and tell our stories through every form of expression available to us.

Shernett has worked with the students of Muhammad

University of Islam in Miami, Florida's performing arts class and over the years she has choreographed such performances entitled, "Origin: 76 Trillion Years of History Revealed", "The Dance of Creation - The Self-Creation of God" and "The Oneness of Allah, God: From a Single Essence He Created the Male and Female."

These performances consist of the very elegance and refined dance "the waltz" also, modern dance, and a dramatic and theatrical performance all of which, depicts aspects of our 76 Trillion years of history as taught by the Most Honorable Elijah Muhammad and the Nation of Islam.

Shernett is a freelance artist whose work ranges from teaching visual and performing art classes to creating decorative art, graphic design, portraits, book illustrations, and murals; including her very vivid detailed conceptual paintings of humanity and nature which, are exhibited in various shows in Miami and Fort Lauderdale, Florida.

SHERNETTART

http://www.shernettart.com/

IN JUSTICE/ DEFENSE

The Home is Our Base, Not Our Place!

SADIYAH A. EVANGELISTA-X
ATTORNEY/ACTIVIST/ EDUCATOR
WIFE & MOTHER/SISTER

Sadiyah Evangelista has been a member of the Texas Bar since April 2002. After graduating from Texas A&M in 1997, she received her Juris Doctorate from Thurgood Marshall School of Law at Texas Southern University in 2001. After graduation politics and social activism came before her practice of law.

Sadiyah served as the Immigration Liaison for Congress-woman Sheila Jackson Lee from 1999-2004, worked for United States President Bill Clinton on his advance team in 1998, and served as Chief of Staff for Council Member Carroll G. Robinson At Large Position 5 from 2001 to

2004. Attorney Evangelista also worked as a Visiting Professor for the Barbara Jordan School of Public Policy for Texas Southern University from 2005 to 2006 teaching undergraduate law related classes.

In 2004, she opened the Law Office of Sadiyah Evangelista and has passionately been working ever since as a criminal defense attorney, specializing in misdemeanors and felonies both on the state and federal level. She is known in her legal community as the "Godly Warrior Lawyer."

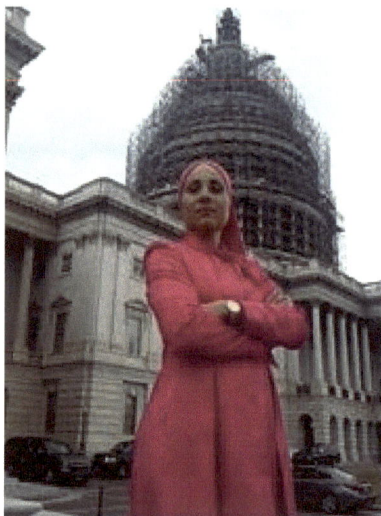

Sadiyah is also the Board President for ACTION CDC - Accepting Challenges To Improve Our Neighborhoods, Community Development Corporation; Co-founder and President of Striving in Society to Achieve Sisterhood (S.I.S.T.A.S) and board member of Respect Inc. In 2015, Sadiyah joined forces with other powerful women to help found, Queendom Come, Inc.. QCI is a non-profit organization with its mission and purpose to empower and elevate women to live her purpose on purpose with grace and finesse as the Queen that she is. Sadiyah is also one of the lead community activists in the Millions More Movement - Ministry of Justice, in which she was involved in publicizing and organizing around the Michael Bell (Jenna Six) case and many others like it locally and nationally.

Sadiyah is married to Kosala Rose-X and is the proud mother of 7.

Hassane Muhammad
ATTORNEY/WARRIOR/ACTIVIST/MOTHER
COO, Black Lawyers For Justice

Tina "Hassane" Muhammad earned her Bachelor of Arts as a Paralegal with a focus on Criminology at Grandview University and graduated Magna Cum Laude. While at Grandview University, Ms. Muhammad started the Black Student Alliance after many incidents of racial indignities occurred on campus. After completing her B.A. at Grandview University, Ms. Muhammad went on to earn her Juris Doctorate from Drake Law School in 2015 with certificates in Constitutional Law and Public Interest Law. She accomplished all of the above, while rearing four active children who between the four of them participated in eleven different extracurricular activities all while she endured the rigors of law school.

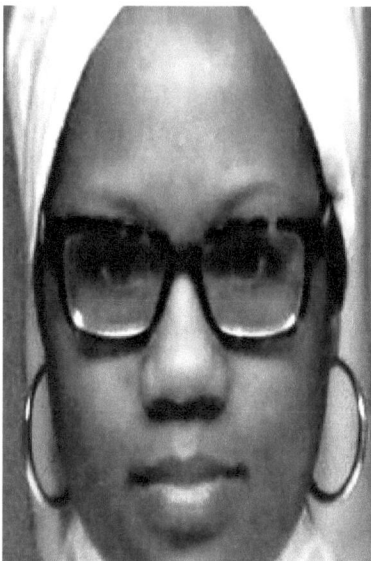

She is currently the founder of "Warrior Law" law firm and Chief Operations Officer at "Black Lawyers for Justice". She also is the founder of a mediation and conflict resolution firm "Mediation Settlement Services" as well as her umbrella company "H&M Consulting and Legal Services, LLC." Dr. Muhammad has traveled throughout the country and internationally on behalf of victims of police brutality and injustice. She has been on the ground in countless demonstrations, protests, and speaking engagements from Ferguson, Missouri all the way to Toronto, Canada. She has helped organize in cities around the country on behalf of "Justice or Else" and "Black Lawyers for Justice". She organized her own city under the banner of "Iowa Citizens for Justice" and conducted a mass rally and town hall meetings in response to the Michael Brown verdict and justice issues suffered locally.

She has served her Nation and her community in various ways since she was a young girl. In high school, she formed P.P.P (Pride, Power and Progress) and organized the Black and minority students at her high school to come together and help out disadvantaged families. Through her leadership they went door to door raising funds and donations to give to disadvantaged families the group adopted. So began a long career of giving back and community involvement. She is proud of organizing and creating a curriculum for her home based school "Elijah Academy" which she opened not only for children in the believing community but also the general community where she taught the students math, science, reading and the teachings of the Most Honorable Elijah Muhammad out of her basement. She also orchestrated and participated in countless community activities focusing on giving back, including: feeding the homeless, organizing clothing and food drives, and mentoring middle school girls through the afterschool program she developed known as P.Y.T (Positive Young Teens).

Dr. Muhammad is a highly sought after Muslim attorney and advocate for Black people, and is known for her firm stance against injustice. She has been interviewed by CNN, BBC, Fox News, NPR, The Carl Nelson Show, Al-Jazeera and countless other radio and television outlets. She has never backed down from her passionate positions against injustice and speaks from the perspective of a Muslim, Mother, an MGT, and a Warrior who has come to terms with the reality that her life and her mission is not her own but for Allah in the service of his people.

She has become successful despite facing personal obstacles and struggles. She knows what it is like to struggle with homelessness and poverty and to be treated unjustly based on race and sex. She has been the victim of sexual harassment and retaliation in the workplace after her white male coworker repeatedly harassed her, she was unjustly fired after reporting the incident. Never to take an injustice lying down, she fought back and won her legal case against her harassers.

She has been the subject of police harassment due to her strong stance against injustice. She has been on the receiving end of death threats and threats of violence to herself and her children by those opposed to the rise of Black people and her strong allegiance to truth and justice. She has been on the streets with protestors, marched on police headquarters, and visited the murder scenes of Mike Brown, Sandra Bland and others, in sometimes dangerous confrontations with the police.

On a daily basis, by Allah's grace and mercy, she answers the calls for justice, listens to heartbreaking stories of injustice, and sees the tears of despair shed by her sisters and brothers whose sons and daughters have been ripped apart by police bullets or given long, unjust prison sentences as part of America's terrorism against Black people. Dr. Muhammad is a courageous, fearless warrior for justice on behalf of her people and gives her life daily to the struggle for freedom, justice and equality. She has made it her mission to defend and uplift those who suffer injustice, and oppression in all of its forms.

WWW.BLFJUSTICE.ORG WWW.WARRIORLAWONLINE.COM

KHALEELAH MUHAMMAD
LEGAL ADVOCATE/COMMUNITY ORGANIZER
ACTIVIST/WRITER/WIFE/MOTHER

Khaleelah Muhammad is a justice advocate, community organizer/activist and writer. Her commitment to literacy and critical thinking also has led her to volunteer her time as a debate coach, curriculum consultant, and spelling bee coordinator. Most recently, she has taught Advanced English (Writing) for the Moraine Valley Community College's GED Program and she volunteers her time working with youth at her local library. Mrs. Muhammad is a wife and mother of three children ranging from elementary school to post-secondary. She grew up in the Englewood and Auburn Gresham communities of Chicago, graduating from Lindblom Technical High School in 1990.

Mrs. Muhammad graduated from Washington University School of Law in St. Louis and was inducted into the Order of Barristers in 2003. She served as an editor for her law school's Journal of Law and Policy. She received the National Association of Public Interest Law Public Service Award and the Dean's Book Award for her service and leadership. Following law school, Mrs. Muhammad directed her passion for advocacy, public policy, teaching and writing into work as a legal writer/editor and a business law and legal research and writing instructor.

She also has served as an area coordinator for the American Bar Association's Law Day Program facilitating *Domestic Violence* and *Know Your Rights Workshops* within the community. Mrs. Muhammad has applied her background in mock trial and moot court to coordinate debate competitions and to work with schools, community organizations and faith communities facilitating dialogues among youth. She was nominated for the Chicago Council on Global Affairs *Emerging Leaders Program* for the Class of 2010-2012.

She recently served as the Project Manager for the Neighborhood Recovery Initiative for the Auburn Gresham Community on behalf of the Faith Community of Saint Sabina. She also served as the Community Representative and Secretary for the Local School Council for South Shore School of Leadership. Mrs. Muhammad served for three years on the Board of ABJ Community Services, headquartered in Chicago's South Shore community, and in her final year, served as Interim Board Chair.

As an advocate in the movement against violence for more than a decade, Mrs. Muhammad has pursued and has been involved in interfaith partnerships. She has served as a Community Ambassador for the Inter Faith Youth Core and the Inner City Muslim Action Network's *One Chicago, One Nation* Program as part of the national *Better Together* Campaign. Mrs. Muhammad works as a resource for and a coalition builder among organizations working to end violence throughout Chicagoland. She has worked with a core group to establish a collaboration between the Ray of Hope Center of the Arts and her mosque. The collaboration provided leadership and character development training for youth and served to produce theatrical productions that utilize their talent and give them a voice to share their perspective on violence and other issues that face youth today.

Mrs. Muhammad founded the *Words Over Weapons* program to optimize outcomes against violence. Committed to collaboration with other anti-violence organizations, Ms. Muhammad annually serves as a judge for the Illinois Council Against Handgun Violence's *Student Voices Competi-*

tion, as a founding member and volunteer of the *Do You Care?* Campaign, and has served both as part of the local Deborah Movement, and early on, with the Prevent School Violence Illinois Coalition. The loss of her younger brother in 2012 and her fellow friend and peace advocate in 2013, both to violence, strengthened her resolve for her work in the movement to end senseless violence and resulted in her pulling together a group of her colleagues and starting the Stringweavers' Peace Initiative in 2013, which continues today.

IN AGRICULTURE & SCIENCE

Beside every great man, walks a great woman!

ANNE MU'MIN MUHAMMAD
COMMUNITY ACTIVIST/ MANAGING PARTNER MU-HAMMAD FARMS, GEORGIA

I was born in Macon, Georgia, September 10, 1949 to the Reverend Willie T. Moore and Mrs. Annie M. Moore. I was educated in the public school system of Bibb County after which I attended Crandall Business College receiving a degree in secretarial Science. I am the mother of one son, Terrence Moore.

At age 19, I began working in my community in Macon, GA, volunteering with many civil rights and social activists organizations. Eventually, I served for seven years as President of the local NAACP chapter.

As a young community activist, I always admired women who were making great strides in helping their communities and society become better places. During those years I met many strong Black women whom I took as mentors in developing my organizational and leadership skills.

I became a Muslim member of the Nation of Islam in 1990 after many years of seeing the same problems being worked on through civil rights and social activism come back around. One night changed my life. I became so distraught when I returned home that night from a community gathering where I had been called to help bring calm after a harmless community drunk was beaten by police. I fell to my knees and prayed and asked God if he too was prejudiced against Black people. I wanted to know why my people were so mistreated by white people.

I cannot recall how long it took after this night for me to make the decision to go to my first Mosque meeting but once I did, I was awe-struck by the wisdom I heard coming from the young minister at that time, Brother Stanley Muhammad (Baatin). After becoming a Muslim, I served as student MGT Captain and Protocol Director at Muhammad Mosque No. 93 in Macon, Georgia.

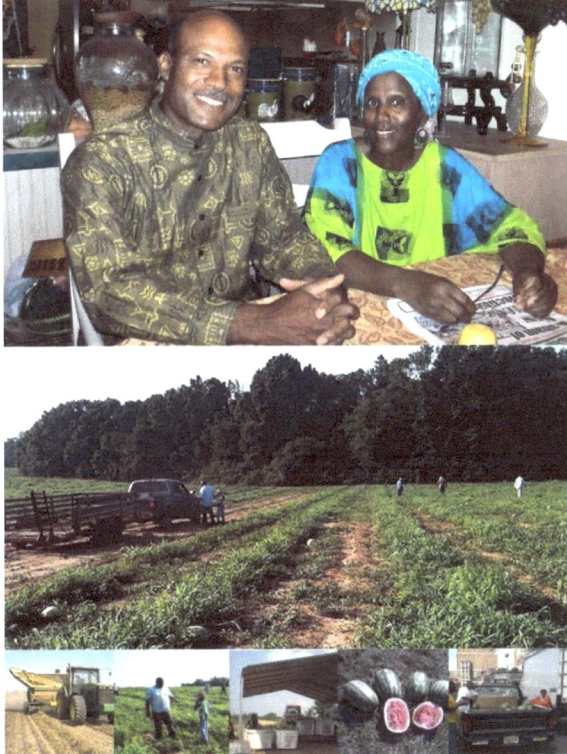

I am now married to Dr. Ridgely A. Mu'min Muhammad who is the Manager of Muhammad Farms in Georgia. A 1600 acre farm purchased by the Honorable Minister Louis Farrakhan, which is part of the original 4500 acre farm purchased by the Most Honorable Elijah Muhammad. Dr. Ridgely, as he is affectionately called is also the National Student Minister of Agriculture for the Nation of Islam. He is an extremely hardworking and dedicated soldier.

Presently, I work alongside my husband in striving to make Muhammad Farms a productive and viable farming operation. To this end, I continue to work in the community and have organized a group of Black women farmers and gardeners who not only grow food but are also contributing to the community by hosting training programs to teach healthy cooking and eating, meal planning, food preservation techniques etc. I also continue to seek knowledge and improve my skills in areas of food preparation and preservation in addition to growing food.

I cannot thank Allah enough for literally saving my life by accepting my prayer to know myself and my people and to gain understanding of how I can be a better servant in helping his chosen servant to resurrect the lost-found nation in the west.

DEBORAH LYNN MUHAMMAD
PHYSICIST TEACHER/ HUMANITARIAN
SCHOLAR/COMMUNITY ACTIVIST
WIFE & MOTHER

Deborah Lynn Muhammad is an educator, workshop facilitator and teacher. She is the author of The Supreme Wisdom Conceptual Curriculum Model: A Transitional Educational Paradigm into the Kingdom of God and many other Supreme Wisdom publications.

Sister Deborah Lynn Muhammad's Accomplishments:

Presenter *The Supreme Wisdom Curriculum: What is it? and How to Design Unit and Lesson Plans*, The Educational Challenge, Houston, TX 2010

Deborah Lynn Muhammad C.E.O., Supreme Educational Wisdom Publishing (S.E.W.) Founder, 2008

Member of the Nation of Islam since 1997

Founding Council Member and Directress of Muhammad University of Islam Baton Rouge Campus since 2003

Nation of Islam National Curriculum Team (Science)

Presenter Curriculum Design Through the Lens of the Teachings of the Most Honorable Elijah Muhammad, Ministry of Education Conference, Chicago, IL 2006

Presenter Unit and Lesson Plans based on the Lessons of Master Fard Muhammad, 1st Annual Nation of Islam Education Conference, Chicago, IL 2007

Presenter Muhammad University of Islam Teacher Professional Development Workshop

How to Teacher Through the Lens of the Teachings of the Supreme Wisdom and the Teachings of the Most Honorable Elijah Muhammad Phoenix, AZ April 4, 2008 Presented By Sister Deborah L. Muhammad

B.A. Journalism, B.S. Physics Education, B.S. Physics

Science Education Center Outreach Coordinator: Caltech University, Laser Interferometer Gravitational Wave Observatory LIGO, Livingston, LA Science Education Center SEC

Workshop Coordinator: Southern University and A&M College, Project MISE Teacher Professional Development

Community Defender TV Live Call-In Talk Show, Co-host

Author and Publisher: Various Education Articles and Documents

Contributing Writer to Final Call Newspaper

Teacher Institute Alumni: San Francisco, CA Exploratorium

Blog Talk Radio – Master Teacher
(http://www.blogtalkradio.com/masterteacher)

IN INFORMATION
MEDIA & PUBLISHING

A Nation Can Rise No Higher Than It's Woman!

"It is time for the woman to come up out of confinement; it is time for the female to glorify God in the greatness of who she is. Women, you've got to be set free... what God has put in you must be cultivated, must be developed, must be used for the advancement of a nation and a world...A New World is to come into existence through you. You are creative women, create things that display you as a highly civilized woman."

—The Honorable Minister Louis Farrakhan
FCN, April 29, 2015

AUDREY MUHAMMAD
PUBLISHER, VIRTUE MAGAZINE/EDUCATOR
FITNESS TRAINER/COLUMNIST
WIFE & MOTHER

Audrey Muhammad is an educator, writer, poet, businesswoman and fitness enthusiast who believes that the original woman is "more valuable than silver and gold" and women should strive to be the epitome of "beauty, class and intelligence."

Mrs. Muhammad is known as an inspirational writer. Her column, "Get Fit to Live," was featured monthly in The Final Call Newspaper for over 10 years and was inspired by Minister Louis Farrakhan's lecture, God's Healing Power, which discussed the importance of exercising. Her column continues to be an inspiration to many. She has always admired Mother Tynnetta Muhammad and was pleased to be a writer in the Final Call along with her. She has received words of praise from Minister Farrakhan commending her for the *Get Fit to Live* Column and *Virtue Today Magazine.*

Mrs. Muhammad has conducted workshops at the Nation of Islam's annual Saviours' day event and in various cities around the country including Los Angeles(LA), Detroit(MI), Oakland(CA), Chicago(IL), Toledo(OH), St. Petersburg(FL), Atlanta(GA), Savannah(GA), Norfork(VA), Richmond(VA), Durham, Greensboro and Charlotte(NC). She has even traveled internationally and has taught workout classes and workshops in St. Croix, Mexico and London, England.

Her magazine, Virtue Today, has been in publication for over a decade and is lovingly called, "The Final Call's Little Sister." Virtue Magazine redefines and displays women with strength, honor, beauty and class. She has interviewed and/or featured Erykah Badu, Mother Tynnetta Muhammad, Mother Khadijah Farrakhan, Dr. Jewel Diamond Taylor, Iyanla Vanzant, Dr. Ava Muhammad, Student Minister Nuri Muhammad and actor, Hill Harper.

The magazine displays beautiful modest fashions, a column by Minister Farrakhan, finance, health and fitness tips. In addition to her magazine, Mrs. Muhammad has also published: *Rhymes of the Times: Black Nursery* Rhymes (a children's book), *The Sister's Guide to Fitness, How to Set Worthy Goals: An Inspirational Guide to Achieving Success* and the book/audiobook, "*Get Fit to Live: Be Your Best You!*

Ms. Muhammad is an Academic Advisor and College Success Instructor. She has a Bachelor of Science Degree in Psychology/Sociology and a Master of Arts in English. As a high school and college educator for the past 20 years, she has learned many techniques to motivate young people. She enjoys teaching kickboxing, yoga and aerobic dance. Her theatre background gave her an opportunity to produce and direct the play, "Tales from the Blackside," which she presented at Bowling Green State University and Michigan State University in the 1990's. She thanks Allah (God) for her family, in particular her daughter, husband and parents, Ernest and Eva Flowers.

She is a dedicated mother, wife and educator who hopes to expand her media business and help enhance our educational system. Her passion for education and fitness has enabled her to travel and inspire others. She has been featured as a guest speaker at the "Living in the Light" women's conference in Arlington, VA, The Black Women's Health and Healing Conference in Oakland, CA, the NAACP's Award Program in Laurinburg, NC and the Health and Wellness conference in London, England(2014). Her presentations have been called, "fun, enlightening, and motivating."

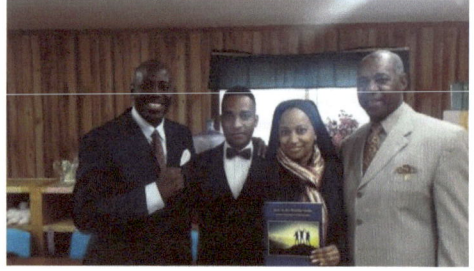

Reach Audrey Muhammad at (510) 815-4591 or at virtuetoday@gmail.com or Virtue Magazine, P.O. Box 61402, Raleigh, NC 27661

CHARLENE MUHAMMAD
JOURNALIST/ RADIO BROADCASTER
NATIONAL CORRESPONDENT/FINAL CALL NEWS
WIFE & MOTHER

Charlene Muhammad is an award-winning multi-media journalist with 18 years of experience in print media and 10 years combined experience in radio broadcast, magazine editing, Internet media and marketing.

Mrs. Muhammad's Internet media and marketing venture, In the Works Media Consultants, grew out of her passion for covering local, national, and international news and views. Web searches for basic information about source organizations was lacking, and she found herself offering write-ups and updates for community-based non-profits who either were abandoned by their web designers, or did not feel they needed web updates, until their businesses began to suffer from the lack of web outreach. Today, her web marketing services include redesign and content management and maintenance, both strengthened by her research/writing ability to tailor original content to each of her client's individual wants and needs.

Mrs. Muhammad began her print career as a freelance then a contributing writer for the *Final Call Newspaper*, published by the Honorable Minister Louis Farrakhan and the Nation of Islam. She was promoted to Staff Writer, then Western Region Correspondent, and to her latest post as National Correspondent for the historical, award-winning publication.

She is founder, host and executive producer of *"Liberated Sisters,"* a weekly program heard every 2nd and 4th Saturday on the Pacifica Network's 90.7 FM/KPFK, *"Uprising: The Freedom Now Edition,"* a drive-time public affairs show heard every Friday morning on the same station, and *"The Justice Report,"* a mini-news segment highlighting various issues, protests, social ills, and the work of advocates and activists to raise awareness and seek justice about those problems.

She is also the founder of *"Pumps on the Ground,"* an independent media project which travels into the trenches, to the scenes of crisis, triumph, advocacy and activism in the Black, White, Indigenous, and underrepresented communities to raise awareness about issues impacting them and their families. She has served as news anchor and field reporter for the KPFK midday and evening newscasts, is a founding member, producer and host of *"Some of Us Are Brave,"* a Black women's radio program (currently on hiatus on KPFK), and worked four years as a producer of 102.3 FM-KJLH Radio's *"Front Page,"* morning public affairs show. There she also produced and hosted the mini-news segment, entitled *"The Next Page,"* which highlighted news overlooked by mainstream media.

Mrs. Muhammad is a contributing writer to the *Los Angeles Sentinel Newspaper* and the *New L.A. Watts Times Newspaper,* and *New America Media*, a nationwide association of over 3000 ethnic media organizations. She's served as Communications Director for *U.S. Doctors for Africa's African First Ladies' Health Summit* as well as for *Project Africa*, a humanitarian HIV/AIDS Mission to Swaziland, South Africa.

SOME AWARDS AND ACCOMPLISHMENTS
> • *Guest Speaker* - "Minority Media Ownership Panel" at the National Association of Black Journalists (NABJ) 35th Anniversary Convention and Career Fair.
> • *Guest Speaker* - The David and Lucile Packard Foundation for Children's Health/New America Media Children's Healthcare Ethnic Media Panel.
> • *Guest Speaker* - "Reporting and Interpreting the News: Keeping It Real and Relevant" Black History Month II Media Panel - The Us Organization.
> • *Recipient* - the "Chronicles of Truth Award," Families to Amend California's Three Strikes and You're Out (F.A.C.T.S.).
> • *Recipient* - "The Ida B. Wells Award in Journalism" from the Mothers for Africa-The Nana Sekyiaabea Foundation.

• *Recipient* - New America Media's Outstanding Reporting on Civil Liberties Issues in Ethnic Communities for Final Call news feature article, "Mother love conquers adversity" on the courage, faith and plight of mothers whose children were killed in police and other gun violence.

• *Recipient* - New America Media Fellowships: 1) 2009 Stimulus Watch Fellowship for Ethnic Media Journalists 2) The David and Lucile Packard Foundation Children's Healthcare Fellowship 3) 2011 Child Poverty 4) Education Beat 2011.

Charlene Muhammad (above) at the 18th Anniversary of the Million Man March in Tuskegee; (right) During F.A.C.T.S. award ceremony at the California African American Museum.

Ms. Muhammad studied Journalism at Southern University A&M College, Baton Rouge, Louisiana, and Public Relations/Journalism at California State University Dominguez Hills, CA. She resides in Carson, California with her husband, Amin Ali Muhammad and their children, Akeila and Mustapha.

EBONY S. MUHAMMAD
PUBLISHER, HURT TO HEALING MAGAZINE
THANATOLOGIST/COUNSELOR/ENTREPRENEUR

Ebony S. Muhammad is a Certified Thanatologist, one who studies death, dying, bereavement, and the psychological means of coping with loss. Ms. Muhammad has her Masters Degree in Psychology from Capella University. She received her Bachelors of Science in Psychology from the University of Houston. Ms. Muhammad's professional background includes Forensic Psychology and general mental healthcare, of which she has assisted clients with Major Depressive Disorder, Bipolar Disorder I, and Schizophrenia Disorder. Ms. Muhammad is also a Certified Professional Dianetics Auditor (Gold Seal).

She is the Publisher of Hurt2Healing Online Magazine, a worldwide publication that offers resolution for real people, which originated from the Hurt to Healing march/rally against domestic violence and sexual assault during the 2006 Essence Festival in Houston, Texas. Hurt2Healing features interviews and article-testimonies from people of diverse backgrounds who have struggled through and overcame the harsh realities of life that many others are suffering from without guidance. Hurt2Healing takes a fearless approach to subject matters that plague both men and women such as drug abuse, abortion, injustice, health/wellness, relationships, entertainment and spirituality.

Ms. Muhammad's area of expertise resides in digital publishing, social media, web design, graphics, photography, research and journalism. Her work has been published in print and digital media outlets such as The Final Call Newspaper, Brother Jesse Blog, Rolling Out Magazine, Bauce Magazine and The Session Magazine. She has been a featured guest on numerous radio shows such as Liberated Sisters (Los Angeles), The Elevated Places (Chicago), Harlem 411 (New York) Majic 102.1 and All Real Radio (Houston).

Her most recent research study, "The Black Male Perspective on Intimacy" (Qualitative), gives an in depth view of Black men, from different walks of life, in intimate relationships and answers the question of whether or not they are interested in having fulfilling relationships with the Black woman.

Ms. Muhammad is also a Licensed Massage & Spa Therapist, Cosmetic Chemist and is the Owner of Origins Massage Spa, the first massage establishment to use food-based products and ingredients in all spa treatments. Her philosophy is, "If it isn't safe enough to eat, why put it on your skin?" She specializes in Deep Tissue, Swedish, Prenatal, Trigger Point, Sports massage, Hot Stone massage, Facial Massage, body wraps and sugar scrub treatments.

IN SPIRITUAL DEVELOPMENT

COMMUNITY SERVICE

Heaven Lies at the Foot of Mother!

ATI HAMID CUSHMERE
HUMANITARIAN/YOUTH ACTIVIST
ARTS, CULTURE, POLITICS EDUCATOR
WIFE & MOTHER

Ati Hamid Cushmeer, who hails from Phoenix, Arizona, now lives in Austin, Texas by way of Atlanta, Georgia where she resided for several years. Since the age of eleven, she has been working her life's purpose: Service to Humanity focusing on Youth through creative use of the Arts, Culture, Politics and Education.

After graduating high school near the top of her class and inducted as a member of the National Honor Society, she attended Arizona State University where she graduated in 1991 with a degree in Political Science with an emphasis on Development in the Middle East and Africa. While there, she served as a delegate in the Model United Nations, served as President/VP of the Black Student Union, and won the crown of Miss Black ASU. She was also one of the founding members of the African-American Student Coalition at ASU, and a member of the student chapter of the NAACP.

Throughout high school, college, and beyond, Ati has served many posts in the Nation of Islam. These include; MGT Treasurer, Lieutenant, Mosque Study Group Coordinator, Youth Study Group Coordinator, Drill Instructor, Vanguard Captain, Honor Guard (Executive Security), acted unofficially as Assistant Minister, served as Mosque Janitor and assisted in answering the hundreds of Nation of Islam (NOI) and Final Call Newspaper online letters.

She has presented at Saviours' Day, served as Youth Representative on the National Council of Laborers (1984-86), The NOI Shura Council, played a leading role in starting the NOI Youth Network (1984-86), organized several committees for Muhammad Mosque #32, led team to develop the MM #32 Resource Directory, organized the Minister's address in Phoenix, AZ (1995), was one of the founding members of the NOI Student Association at Arizona State, developed the NOISA Policy Manual (1996), and a Policy and Procedure Manual for Mosque #32. She has represented the Nation before many groups. Of them; El Partido de la Raza Conference, traveled to the Native American Ceremony "Stand at Big Mountain," and the Black Youth Recognition Conference, of which she volunteered and presented for over 13 years.

Professionally, she has worked extensively for young people as Program Director for the newly created Urban Services at the YMCA, Title 19 Counselor, Youth (Gang) Specialist, Probation Officer, Youth Program Coordinator (specializing in community development) as Administrative Coordinator/Program Manager at the Fulton County Juvenile Court in Atlanta, Georgia. In this position, Ati developed community collaborations and partnerships between the Court and community based organizations/government departments; grant writing, management and compliance, prepare & oversee budgets; write policy, research and analysis, track legislation, chaired and served on coalitions including court gang task force, project management, supervised staff/volunteers, and oversaw Court programs; and was a registered Georgia Mediator (General/Juveniles).

HIGHLIGHTS
-Established the Court's Community Service/Restitution Program
-Interfaith Children's Movement of Metro Atlanta (Member) -a collaboration across religious lines to address major issues among youth & families
-Initiated & Chaired Latino Advisory Council to increase diversity/understanding to better serve Latino youth and families in the Court.
-Initiated the Fulton County Coalition to End Child Trafficking/Commercial sexual exploitation. This effort grew in leadership and later resulted in stronger legislation, state, national and international information sharing & the development of a continuum of care for victims (OJJDP

Demonstration Project).

-Served on OJJDP Child Exploitation Demonstration Project

-Assisted Director in program development for the Juvenile Justice Fund (Foundation) develops collaborations and partnerships between community organizations, government agencies and the Court, chairs coalitions, project and program management, grant writing/compliance, track legislation, research and analysis.

First participating in the Cynthia McKinney Sister to Sister Delegation in 1999, Ati later volunteered for former Congresswoman Cynthia McKinney (Georgia, 4th District) from 2002-2003 and later served on her Executive Team and worked as a Volunteer Coordinator (2003-2004).

Other highlights while living in Atlanta include serving on the Tavis Smiley's Youth II Leaders planning committee, participating in the United Way VIP Board Development program and in 1998, Ati served as President of the "Million Youth Movement" held in Atlanta, Georgia. This three day convention included a Youth Town Hall, Hip-Hop Poetry Party, Gospel Concert in collaboration with the Youth USA Achievement Awards, Interfaith Service, Workshops, and a Rally.

As an avid volunteer and activist, Ati has worked among young people in gangs, the homeless, as a mentor and community neighborhood revitalization projects. She was part of the "Youth for Jesse Jackson" Presidential Campaign, Citizens for Improved Police Relations Coalition (Phoenix, AZ), Self-Expression Theater Ensemble, the Phoenix and later, Atlanta MMM Local Organizing Committee and is a life time member of the (NCNW) National Council for Negro Women, Millennium Chapter.

She has been the recipient of several awards including "Three Outstanding Young Phoenicians," "1996 Youth Advocate," "2002 NCNW Bethune Recognition Award" for community service, and was twice nominated "Outstanding Atlantan."

She has served as a Mediator and is experienced in the U.S. Census (including the special count for the homeless/under-represented populations), skilled in public speaking, program development, and as a trainer in various areas. In 2004, Ati organized the development of the Healthy Relationships Initiative (HRI) with a team of volunteers. The purpose of HRI is strengthening families via marriage preparation and developing a healthy relationship with God, self, family, friends and spouses. Since 2004, retreats have been held all over the United States and have inspired others to develop similar initiatives.

Upon getting married in 2009, Ati relocated to Austin, Texas where she is now a Mother and is working on the management team for R&B artist, Nubia Emmon, who is also her step-daughter. In this capacity, Ati is a Special Projects Specialist. She handles; all aspects of marketing and promotions, web design and maintenance, event planning and she is spearheading the development of the Nubia Emmon Foundation which is focused on advocating for breast cancer awareness and motivating youth toward success. Ati is also very much involved in the "Justice or Else" movement and toward that end, she is currently planning a major national Family Summit along with a team of volunteers.

Ati is looking forward to working on an international level as well as relocating back to Phoenix with her family. She enjoys the Fine Arts (dance, acting, painting) and her hobbies include reading, poetry, hiking, traveling, fitness, and political participation.

RUTH MUHAMMAD
WIFE & MOTHER/HOME-MAKER
HUMANITARIAN/COMMUNITY ACTIVIST

Through the teachings of the Most Honorable Elijah Muhammad, as exemplified by the Honorable Louis Farrakhan, I have learned the true meaning of being a Muslim
wife, mother, sister and humanitarian. I have learned the
true sense of their meaning and purpose in my life. Our
M.G.T. and G.C.C. has helped me to see the real values of
being a good wife and the importance of our homemaker
role. I find both rewarding. It is rewarding to be a wife
and a good mother. The woman is the first teacher and it
is very important for me to be a teacher of my family. The

teachings of the Most Honorable Elijah Muhammad have taught me to value myself as a woman who carries herself with the highest standards and no longer desires to disrespect myself.

The Honorable Elijah Muhammad teaches us that to teach a woman is to teach a nation. I realize how important it is to impart this message to my children. I know that my role is great in the eyes of Allah. The teachings of the Honorable Elijah Muhammad have taught me there is value in all of us. Being a homemaker is absolutely an important job in my family. I love seeing my children's talents and development. It gives me great joy to assist my husband, a man of God, to become the best Muslim. I am also happy to observe our sisters come into this teaching and training and develop into good Muslims.

Islam has made me more aware of our peoples' struggle, and to know that the blame for our condition is not all our fault. Our condition is because of the harsh realties we face in this system. Before Islam, I saw our people differently. It has shown me the value of myself. I am more conscious and in tune with myself, always striving to be righteous. I give strong focus on my own personal growth and development.

My journey to the Nation of Islam came as a result of my husband, Student Minister Stanley Muhammad. He introduced me to the Honorable Minister Louis Farrakhan through one of his lectures. Later, I recall attending a talent show, where I met an MGT. I became a Muslim the first time I came to the mosque. What was being taught agreed with my soul. It connected with me so I began to study Islam and the teachings of the Most Honorable Elijah Muhammad. I officially joined in 1990. It has been a beautiful journey that as I have encountered the trials of life I have been able to overcome because I see them through the eyes of God.

Nayyirah Tivicia Muhammad
Humanitarian/Community Activist/ life skills coach/auditor/wife & mother

The Local M.G.T. & G.C.C. Sister Student Captain in St. Petersburg, Florida for Nation of Islam's Muhammad's Mosque # 95, is moving throughout communities offering her training, skills, and talents as a Life Skills Coach and Motivational Speaker. With divine guidance from the Honorable Minister Louis Farrakhan she forges the way to happiness and success.

As a former four year local NAACP President of the Youth Council, board member of Youth on the Move, Prison Ministry Reform member, and member of the National Council of Negro Women, Sister Nayyirah Tivica Muhammad counsels youth by speaking at high schools and girls homes, participates in Interfaith dialogues with community faith organizations, and has hosted Women's Conferences with guest speakers and National figures: Sister Donna Farrakhan and Sister Student Minister Ava Muhammad.

She can be heard monthly on her radio show on the Hereafter is Now Network. Mrs. Muhammad has received the designation of the first Superpower Completion in the Nation of Islam along with the following distinguished awards and training: Dianetics Gold Seal H.D.A. Auditor,

President's Volunteer God Service Award, the Amanda Ambrose Soldier of the Heart Award, 2020 Plan Taskforce Spokesperson Award, Teen Mom Award, and the NAACP Parent Community Award. Above all, Sister Nayyirah Tivica Muhammad, creates heaven on earth for her husband of 16 years, Brother Dawud Muhammad, her five beautiful children, and her grandson Nadir.

WORLD CLASS AMBASSADORS & LEADERSHIP

M.G.T. & G.C.C. and Vanguard Class Photo
Mosque Maryam
Chicago, Illinois

Notable Women Figures in the Nation of Islam
Past & Present

MOTHERS OF THE FAITHFUL
MOTHER CLARA MUHAMMAD
MOTHER TYNNETTA MUHAMMAD
MOTHER KHADIJAH FARRAKHAN MUHAMMAD
MOTHER EVELYN MUHAMMAD
MOTHER OLA MUHAMMAD

DAUGHTERS OF THE HONORABLE MINISTER LOUIS FARRAKHAN
SISTER DONNA FARRAKHAN MUHAMMAD
SISTER FATIMAH FARRAKHAN MUHAMMAD
SISTER MARIA FARRAKHAN MUHAMMAD
SISTER BETSY JEAN FARRAKHAN MUHAMMAD
SISTER KALLADA FARRAKHAN MUHAMMAD

NATIONAL MUSLIM WOMEN FIGURES & REPRESENTATIVES
SISTER SANDY MUHAMMAD, STUDENT NATIONAL CAPTAIN MGT

SISTER MINISTER AVA MUHAMMAD, ATTORNEY, NATIONAL SPOKES-
PERSON, FOR THE HONORABLE MINISTER LOUIS FARRAKHAN

SISTER A'ISHAH MUHAMMAD, STUDENT NATIONAL AUDITOR COORDI-
NATOR & STUDENT NATIONAL MGT CAPTAIN EMERITUS

MARY ALICE MUHAMMAD, LEAD CHEF FOR THE HONORABLE MIN-
ISTER LOUIS FARRAKHAN

REGIONAL CENTERS OF LEARNING FOR THE MGT & GCC
SOUTHERN (ATLANTA, GEORGIA)
SOUTHWEST (HOUSTON, TX)
WESTERN (LOS ANGELES, CA)
CARIBBEAN (7TH) (MIAMA, FL)
MID-ATLANTIC & EASTERN (WASHINGTON, D.C. & NEW YORK)
UNITED KINGDOM (LONDON)
CANADA (TORONTO, MONTREAL)
FRANCE (PARIS)

WE ARE OUR SISTER'S KEEPERS!

-What is A Sister?-

1. A female having the same parents as another or on er or one parent in common with another.

2. A girl or woman who shares a common ancestry, allegiance, character, or purpose with another or er or others, specifically:

a. A kinswoman.

b. A woman fellow member, as of a sorority.

c. A fellow woman.

d. A close woman friend or companion.

e. A fellow African-American woman or girl.

f. A woman who advocates, fosters, or takes part in the feminist [sic] womanist movement.

3. *Informal* Used as a form of address for a woman or girl.

4. *Abbr.* **Sr.** *Ecclesiastical*

a. A member of a religious order of women; a nun.

ABOUT

On Top of the World: Profiles in Courage - Women of the Nation of Islam is a collection of narratives and facts about the Soldiers, Scholars, Wives, Mothers, Sisters, Students and Servants who live, work and serve their families, communities, black people, this nation and the world. Their lives demonstrate a true exercise of agency. From all walks of life, the Muslim Girls Training & General Civilization Class produces some of the most renowned Sister Servants in the U.S. They represent one of the greatest ambassador forces assembled under the spiritual, cultural and economic umbrella of The Nation of Islam. Based on their current roles and involvement in the political, social justice and cultural movements of the day, the M.G.T. & G.C.C. will have a great impact on the condition and empowerment of people of color in the United States, and the World, for generations to come. This book offers a glimpse, a peek into the caliber of women that come out of the class known affectionately as the MGT!

ABOUT THE AUTHOR
DR. TONI S. MUHAMMAD

PROFESSOR/ SCHOLAR/ MENTOR
SERVANT LEADER / COMMUNITY ACTIVIST

Dr. Toni S. Muhammad a master teacher, higher education career spans 25 years with faculty positions held at colleges and universities in Louisiana, Illinois, North Carolina and Georgia. She holds a Bachelor and Masters Degree in Sociology and a Doctor of Arts in Humanities with an ethnic studies concentration in African and African American Studies from Clark Atlanta University. She is one of the first women in the United States to complete a dissertation about the notions of womanhood in the Nation of Islam. She is a trailblazer and torchbearer for Muslim (and non-Muslim) girls and women inside and outside of the classroom. She is known and respected by her students and colleagues for her tireless mentoring and service toward academic excellence. She is married to her biggest supporter, Tarik, and has four amazing and beautiful children Tynetta, Ava, Amir and Kaeed. She lives in the metro Atlanta area where she currently teaches at Kennesaw State University in the African and Africana Diaspora Studies Program.

ABOUT THE EDITOR

NISA I. MUHAMMAD

WEDDED BLISS FOUNDATION/ DEEN INTENSIVE ACADEMY
JOURNALIST/HUMANITARIAN/ACTIVIST

Staff writer for The Final Call Newspaper and Fashion Editor for Azizah Magazine, Nisa Muhammad was featured on CNN's "Black in America 2". Her groundbreaking work with the Wedded Bliss Foundation showcased her healthy marriage education for Black couples throughout the country. Nisa also is the creator of the Ramadan Prayer Line and works with her husband, Abdul Jalil Muhammad, with the Deen Intensive Academy.

What is the Meaning of M.G.T. & G.C.C.?

Ans. - Muslim Girl Training and Civilization Class. How to Keep House, How to Rear Our Children, How to Take Care of Our Husbands, Cook, sew and in general how to act at home and abroad. These seven training units were given to us by our leader and teacher of Islam, W. D. Fard.

The duty of an MGT is to reflect the highest moral and ethical standards in character and behavior. We the MGT represents the best manifestation that GOD appeared in the person of Master Fard Muhammad, taught and elevated the Most Honorable Elijah Muhammad and gave to the world a Divine Reminder and Warner, the Honorable Louis Farrakhan Muhammad.

www.ingramcontent.com/pod-product-compliance
Lightning Source LLC
Chambersburg PA
CBHW040804280326
41926CB00082B/17